the myths I miss the most

Aurelia Lee

BookLeaf Publishing

India | USA | UK

Presentation by *BookLeaf Publishing*

Web: www.bookleafpub.com

E-mail: info@bookleafpub.com

ISBN:9789358317688

First edition 2024

DEDICATION

for myself, and the bravery it took to forsake faith and find freedom.

ACKNOWLEDGEMENT

to all the scars, secrets, and strength I have carried thus far: thank you.

the myth i miss the most

the myth i miss the most
parted pages and seas
rivers run red
a plague upon houses that mysteriously missed
my head
and I was protected, sanctified, and fed.
imagined curses danced past my lips
honey drip
wine split
venom visiting veins;
i pray for enemies they told me existed
sweat rolls off my victim complex.
i yearned to be oppressed
i lapped the lines of propaganda;
forcing birth
lesser worth
i know my place under His heel.
storm outside
storm within
peace punctured by legalism
save your tears for the sermon
i'm not depressed under His eye.
and yet
the halls swell and sway
arches crafted to catch the songs,

my voice
is not alone, but builds and breaks
on long nights and colder days;
i found the sound before i found my faith.
the myth i miss the most
raised and raged for me
a cherished champion
i cannot be alone in the dark if He placed in me
the light
He would hear my withered whimpers in the day
or night.
solitary singing
penitent praise
I walked away --
echoes forming over feet and heart
stones for eyes
i drink deeply with no blood
just wine.
all mine.

primus

heads hanging, hunched in a row
chairs stacked like teeth
being bitten by disbelief.
we bow to decorated walls
air escapes our lips
is this prayer? or am I
a victim of fiction?

and I said
what if we are alone?

secundus

hope whispered in the dark
but the dark was asleep
and my mind made answers for me.
don't dare to question the Son
rising over the hills
casting shadows between
the heads of the suffering

and I said
I think we are alone

tertius

5

the trusted canticle for centuries
a longing to be loved
the fatherless and the bruised
drawn to the music
a salty sweet hymn
desperate for a drop of acceptance

and I said --
I know we are alone.

the good kid

I did not want to be held
but I wanted to be known.
so a god was perfect for me.

Spending hours in the quiet
feeding on my isolation.
reading, praying - and they were proud of me.
despondent, devoted, dependent was I;
building a heaven instead of a home.

the world cuts at the corners
i'm nascent and groaning.
needing to believe the lord loved me.

giving me more than I can handle

it is well with my soul.

the good book said he was a jealous god
and that was my introduction to love.

it is well with my soul.

there is no deep breathing in the scripture
instead, vengeful bursts
righteous, of course,
because virulence belongs to the gods.

it is well with my soul.

a bone needs to be broken to set and heal
but why was I snapped again and again
as though pain
was for the pleasure of a god.

it is not well with my soul
it is not well with my soul
it is not well with the whole of my soul

all men

grab em by the
  grab em by
    grab em
      grab

not something wanted, but expected, they say
under stadiums surrounded by men and sweat.
watching deacons and wise women
defend an ascertain of ownership
"all men talk like that"
all men?
I'm locked in the pew,
headlines running in my head
wondering who:
the grandfathers guiding the next generation?
a father with five mouths to feed?
the fresh-married pastor?
assaulting me with one hand and turning bible
pages with the other?
I walk
between the aisles and wonder
which one of these men is the same:
who describes their wife to their friends this way

who hopes someone does that to his daughter
one day
who imagines his mother invites such behavior
who expects his sister to accept propositions.
I chew communion with racing thoughts,
fold my arms over my lap
disembodied parts
replace bride of the church with meat for the
feast
is that all i am to
all of these men?
their savior commends it --
a liar, an adulterer, an assaulter, a crude monster
speaking ill and death to the least of these
mocking and maiming lost sheep.
"all men talk like that".

the man to the left of me coughs
I inch farther away
if all men would debase me
what good is their god.
if all men would hate me
then who should I trust.

grab em by the
        grab em by
                grab em
                        grab

submission is not a dirty word, but

mountains never made by me
dragging, crawling,
stubborn hands and bleeding knees
social graces tasting plates
first smooth and sweet
but bitter when aged
no more opinions when a husband needs

wedding night

took three tries

three nights

three reassurances

a holy number
divine, perhaps?
father, son, holy spirit
blood, pain, and disappointment

waited my whole life just to hate this.

gift

the first time I sang, I sang for god
and it echoed back through
empty halls, with windows
stained and stolen.
told myself the space was peace,
was breath inside lungs
or the pause between heartbeats
instead of unanswered air.
The first time I wrote, I wrote for god
and words flowed as water
deep streams, fast currents
that swept me somewhere else.
filled the silence with prayer,
speech inspired, bubbling
from somewhere below
that they told me was holy.
The first time I loved, I loved for god.
and because I promised before Him
i could not let it go -
not even when song and word
turned into ash streaked across my forehead.

ouroboros

13

you should not need a god
to keep impulses in check.

you should not have impulses
to hurt and harm others.

you should not hurt and harm others
in the name of a god.

resurrect

my past hands
calloused from throwing stones
my printed pages
support a black and white story
my untangling of sin
from the trappings of self
my already prepared
to leave a world I had barely begun.

make me

I never want to be a god.
prayer passes through smoke before it gets to me
jealous
anxious
vengeful
dirty;
all love make me feel like a fraud.
but
maybe if i was a god
maybe if i claimed a name,
an ancient book
could overflow
with my fabricated please and sobs.
burned fingers twitch
tied tongue smites
to plunder and rule, and then you'd fight
to keep me unfettered and free
dining on the rights of my enemies.
paper pages resuscitated while
those with souls and skins bleed.
but
maybe if i was a god
maybe if i made the world.

Sunday

Wednesday was the day i thought for myself
mind cracked like a book
(at least one of us has a spine)
study in return for presumption
telling others to live life incomplete.
it wasn't a choice for me.

Thursday, another afternoon, laid to waste
striking walls with my heels
(i'm pacing faster than this morning)
one end of the room a phone flashes
a divine duty even though it hurts.
he'll never love me as christ loved the church.

Friday has become a sample of sin
twenty-five years in the making
(laced tight up the back, to the top of my head)
i knit everything closed under a loose sweater.
clay without purpose, body made for temptation
carving it up never makes the sensations fade.

Saturday, rapid fire from a loose barrel mouth
am i innocent? no. am i pure? hardly.
(he left my apartment in the afternoon)
this time the phone flashes from a distance

I've no need of covenants constructed from
scraps
this week knocked something loose, i can't put it
back.

Sunday.

at home for the first time.

upturned flowers on a counter greet me
goodmorning,

if this is sin, I'm doomed.

give me a sign

my mind is a graveyard where I bury my doubt.

I want to ask questions but they need more salt.

what if - i am formless without this - am I

bitter and burnt out and unknown.

Bartimeus

have faith

have faith

believe in what you never see

fingers dug into my eyes

still i'm following blindly.

have faith

have faith

crusades never named the suffering

stained glass bathes me in light

while others burn and swing.

have faith

have faith

I think my divine protection

is just the name of my god

or the color of my skin.

have an eye for an eye

I see what I want to see.

equal

humans are capable, creative, and cruel.
cycles of hatred or
endings dipped in healing;
both drip from all lips.
without faith the sun rips open a new day,
while wounds heal regardless of prayer.
sons are born and fathers die
by battlefield or slumber
maidens turn to mothers, and mothers to crones.
all things bloom and wither.
we need the dirt but it does not need us.
when water has vanished, thirsty faith
to quench us in theory but parched tongues bleed
still.
there is no need for a creed -
life pushes up in the soil.
we are visitors here, not masters.

vessel speaking

bear a child or bear a curse
30 days until i go in the dirt
i can feel where the knife twists and turns
hold my hand and my head
it's gonna hurt.
let the man measure your worth.
it's gonna hurt.
pay no heed to mother earth.
it's gonna hurt.
women made men and man made god.

it's gonna hurt.
the life I could have ignored
a vessel waiting for something more
as though my choice weren't worth fighting for
and beneath the grave the voices pour.
women made men and man made god.

it's coming undone
matriarchs wail just before the dawn
under my feet a rage has spawned
shadows of mothers and daughters gone
grief whittles my teeth and wets my gums.
women made men and man made god.

it yearns to be free
I am not the vessel they made out of me.
women made men and man made god
to pretend to have power over what i could be.

prosperity gospel

I am not the earth
The Earth thinks that it is me
veins and streams bubble before hitting the rocks
moss and skin darken under embrace from the
sun.
I was created to trample and toil
crushed nests with skyscrapers and
the oceans are choking on plastic containers
they told me to sweat for my place in the pew.
work hard and see god.

i am not the earth
The Earth dares to defy me
six days, then creation
to happily rise and grind and take what is mine.
five days later, then flora and fauna
must move aside for private planes
I escalate, heat rises, the dollar inflates;
millions of years to create
just one to inspire extinction.
hunt hard and see god.

i am not the earth
The Earth is a conspiracy
simpering sadness soyboys created

rules to constrain my gain.
i must grow unfettered

keep going
keep building
keep plowing
keep draining
keep slaughtering
keep colonizing
keep destroying
I must have my burgers and
I must have my mansions and
I must have five divorces and
I'll tell you what blessed is.
lie hard and see god.

recovery

when the day grew dim i took a walk beside
myself
to see what i could see.
I had not noticed the slant of my nose or the roll
of my chin
for quite some time.
i used to regard my body with fear, with distrust,
when would my impulses
next betray me?
control given in small bites, in counting ribs and
collarbones
fasting is godliness.
for god was abundance, and i should be
humbled,
consuming less praying more.
now i wiggle and wave, wandering hands over
waterfall curves,
unapologetic and abundant.
i think i have made myself a map, scarves and
dimples carving a path
no sin on the horizon.
he's in my bed, she's in my thoughts, and room
for all my wants
hell is not a place but stasis.

no iniquity in bleeding, breeding, or feeding --
my body is mine
i recover it.

the myth i missed the most

the myth i missed the most
gave way to a sense of safety in myself.
would pain be satiated if my love had been less?
could the road be smooth if covered in rules?
what does regret taste like under the tongue?
questions boil where faith had once been.
my mind buzzes,
the bees set free
drip both venom and honey over me.
if there is a consequence,
i will embrace it
heartbreak is acceptance
instead of penitence.
my choices rain freely
a drizzle
a storm
a flood
there is no ark; i swallow it whole.
will i drown if my fear rises from the waves?
can i still walk on water with my faith?
shall I freely swim
head over and under
baptised in free will,
and be consumed by a life well lived.
above me,

stars for eyes.
i missed the communion
i drink deeply with no blood
just wine.
all mine.